COLLINS KOLE

Apogee of the Quantum Wanderer

Contents

1

Anomalies Unveiled

The quantum lab hummed with a rhythmic pulse as Dr. Elara Quinn meticulously prepared for her groundbreaking experiment. She adjusted the dials on the imposing quantum generator, its metallic surface shimmering with an ethereal glow. The air crackled with anticipation as Elara initiated the entanglement sequence.

As the quantum particles danced in orchestrated chaos, Elara noticed a subtle shift in the room's energy. An anomaly, small but palpable, echoed through the laboratory. It was as if reality itself had taken an imperceptible step sideways.

Elara furrowed her brow, scrutinizing the data streaming across the holographic display. The readings were unprecedented, defying the established laws of quantum mechanics. Her heartbeat quickened with a mix of excitement and trepidation.

Unbeknownst to Elara, surveillance cameras recorded every nuance of her experiment. In a dimly lit control room, a mysterious figure observed her every move with an intensity that sent shivers down their spine. Shadows concealed their features, leaving only the glint of watchful eyes.

As Elara delved deeper into the entanglement, the anomalies multiplied. Quantum particles seemed to communicate in ways unaccounted for by conventional physics. Whispers of uncertainty filled the air, as if the fabric of reality itself was testing the boundaries of its own existence.

The laboratory lights flickered, casting eerie shadows on the walls. Elara, absorbed in her work, remained oblivious to the growing tension in the room. The quantum generator pulsated with increasing vigor, its glow intensifying as if drawing energy from the very fabric of the universe.

A sudden gust of wind swept through the lab, extinguishing the flickering lights. In the ensuing darkness, Elara felt a presence, an intangible force that lingered on the periphery of her awareness. Her instincts screamed at her to halt the experiment, but an insatiable curiosity urged her forward.

The holographic display flashed with erratic patterns, resembling a cosmic ballet of entangled particles. Elara's hands trembled as she reached for the emergency shutdown switch, but before she could act, a voice resonated through the chamber. A voice that seemed to transcend the boundaries of time itself.

"Unravel the mysteries, Elara Quinn, for the quantum dance has just begun."

The voice echoed, resonating with a melodic yet haunting cadence. Elara's breath caught in her throat as the words hung in the air, leaving an indelible imprint on her consciousness.

The surveillance figure in the control room leaned closer to the screen, a sinister grin playing on their lips. The unseen observer reveled in the unfolding chaos, their connection to Elara's experiment veiled in the quantum shadows.

As the final echoes of the mysterious voice faded, the lab plunged into silence.

Elara stood alone amidst the remnants of her experiment, acutely aware that she had ventured into uncharted territory. The anomalies, like enigmatic breadcrumbs, beckoned her to explore the uncharted depths of the quantum realm, setting in motion a series of events that would unravel the very fabric of her understanding.

2

The Unseen Observer

The following day, Elara Quinn couldn't shake the eerie feeling that lingered from the enigmatic voice. Her laboratory, once a haven of scientific inquiry, now bore an atmosphere thick with unspoken secrets. As she sifted through the data logs from the previous night's experiment, anomalies jumped out at her, each more confounding than the last.

A persistent itch of paranoia settled upon Elara's skin, prompting her to scrutinize the surveillance footage. The screens flickered to life, revealing the sterile lab bathed in the ghostly glow of quantum particles. As she reviewed the recordings, her eyes widened at a revelation - subtle distortions, imperceptible to the naked eye, riddled the footage.

Someone had been watching her, someone with a vantage point beyond the confines of the observable universe. The unseen observer, hinted at by the mysterious voice, had left their digital footprints in the surveillance system. Elara's heartbeat quickened as she traced the anomalies back to their source.

In a dimly lit corner of the lab, she discovered a hidden camera, its lens pointed directly at the quantum generator. Anger and unease coiled within her, for this intrusion cut deeper than a mere breach of privacy. Someone, or something, had infiltrated the very heart of her research.

Determined to uncover the truth, Elara enlisted the help of her colleague, Dr. Marcus Turner, an expert in cybersecurity. Together, they delved into the labyrinth of digital signatures, tracing the electronic breadcrumbs left by the unseen observer. The lab's computers hummed with activity as they unraveled the layers of encryptions.

As the night wore on, the duo's investigations led them down a rabbit hole of conspiracy and clandestine machinations. The surveillance system breach wasn't an isolated incident; it was part of a broader network of covert monitoring, reaching far beyond the confines of their quantum research.

Marcus, his eyes widened in disbelief, whispered, "This goes deep, Elara. Someone has been manipulating the very foundations of our reality."

The revelation sent shivers down Elara's spine. The quantum experiments, once confined to the realm of scientific exploration, now danced on the precipice of something far more profound - a cosmic chess game where the pieces were human lives and the stakes, the fabric of existence itself.

As dawn painted the sky in hues of pink and gold, Elara and Marcus found themselves on the brink of a revelation. The surveillance network, intricately woven into the fabric of the quantum lab, had its tendrils extending into governmental agencies, shadowy organizations, and uncharted territories of the digital realm.

With the first light of day, a chilling realization settled upon Elara – she was not merely unraveling the mysteries of the quantum realm; she was entangled in a web of intrigue that spanned dimensions beyond her comprehension. The unseen observer, their gaze fixated upon her work, had set in motion a chain of events that threatened not only the boundaries of science but the very essence of her existence.

3

Echoes of Tomorrow

A restless night followed Elara's discovery of the unseen observer's intrusion. Sleep eluded her as she grappled with the weight of revelations that stretched the boundaries of her understanding. As dawn painted the horizon in muted hues, Elara found herself drawn back to the quantum lab, an insatiable thirst for answers burning within her.

The holographic display flickered to life as she reinitiated the quantum generator, the soft hum resonating through the laboratory. As the quantum particles danced in orchestrated chaos, Elara closed her eyes, seeking a connection to the elusive mysteries that now intertwined with her research.

In the depths of her mind, a kaleidoscope of images unfolded – visions of a future yet to come. Dystopian landscapes sprawled before her, cities reduced to rubble, and skies painted in ominous hues. The quantum entanglement had become a conduit to the future, and Elara found herself standing at the crossroads of destiny.

A voice, hauntingly familiar, whispered through the quantum currents. "The choices you make echo through time, Elara Quinn. The future is but a reflection of the paths you tread."

The enigmatic words lingered, leaving Elara with a sense of foreboding. The visions continued, revealing glimpses of divergent timelines shaped by her decisions. Each choice, a pebble cast into the pond of time, created ripples that reverberated through the tapestry of existence.

Drenched in a cold sweat, Elara staggered back from the holographic display. The implications of her experiments reached far beyond the confines of scientific curiosity. She held within her grasp the power to shape the future, and with that power came the burden of responsibility.

Unable to shake the weight of the visions, Elara sought solace in the dimly lit corners of her office. The walls, adorned with equations and quantum diagrams, seemed to close in on her. The boundaries between present and future blurred, and she grappled with the realization that the quantum realm was not just a canvas for scientific exploration but a tapestry of fate itself.

In the midst of her contemplation, a knock echoed through the door. Dr. Felix Arden, a renegade physicist with a reputation for pushing the boundaries of conventional science, stood on the threshold. His eyes, sharp and perceptive, met Elara's with a knowing gaze.

"I've been following your work, Dr. Quinn. The quantum entanglement experiments have caught the attention of those who understand the true potential of such discoveries," Felix remarked cryptically.

Elara, still reeling from the revelations, regarded him with a mix of suspicion and curiosity. Felix, sensing her internal struggle, extended an offer.

"Come with me, Elara. There are truths beyond the veil of academia, and together, we can unravel the mysteries that transcend the boundaries of time."

The choice loomed before her – the safety of the known or the allure of the unknown. As the quantum generator pulsed with anticipation, Elara stood at the precipice of a journey that would redefine not only her understanding of science but her very place within the tapestry of existence.

4

Entangled Alliances

The corridors of the research facility echoed with an ethereal hush as Elara Quinn followed Dr. Felix Arden into uncharted territory. A clandestine meeting room awaited, its walls adorned with holographic displays flickering in hues of quantum uncertainty. Felix's gaze, unwavering, met Elara's as he began to unveil the mysteries that had drawn him to her work.

"Elara, what you've uncovered goes beyond the boundaries of conventional science. The entanglement experiments have breached the veil between realities," Felix explained, his words carrying a weight that resonated with both excitement and caution.

As holographic schematics danced in the air, Felix revealed a device of intricate design – a quantum navigator. It was the key to traversing the boundaries of parallel universes, a technology rumored to exist only in the shadowy fringes of scientific exploration.

"The Quantum Navigator allows us to manipulate the entanglement field, opening gateways to alternate realities. But beware, Elara, for with each step into the unknown, we risk unraveling the delicate threads that hold our own reality together," Felix cautioned, his eyes reflecting the gravity of their undertaking.

Intrigued and apprehensive, Elara contemplated the possibilities. The unseen observer, the mysterious voice, and the surveillance network – all threads converging in a tapestry of cosmic intrigue. With a nod of determination, she embraced the alliance with Felix, recognizing that the answers to her questions lay in the uncharted territories they were about to explore.

The duo embarked on a journey through the quantum corridors, navigating the entanglement fields with the Quantum Navigator as their guide. Reality blurred as they traversed the delicate balance between existence and nonexistence. Each step opened gateways to parallel universes, revealing worlds where the laws of physics diverged and the familiar gave way to the fantastical.

In one reality, they encountered a society advanced beyond imagination, harnessing quantum energies for utopian purposes. In another, a desolate wasteland where the echoes of a cataclysmic event resonated through the air. Elara, wide-eyed and awe-inspired, began to grasp the vastness of the quantum multiverse.

Yet, with every leap between realities, subtle nuances emerged. Whispers of dissonance echoed through their journey, hinting at an underlying instability in the fabric of the quantum realm. As the Quantum Navigator hummed with increasing intensity, Elara and Felix faced a dilemma – the very act of exploration threatened to unravel the delicate balance of the entanglement fields.

Amidst the cosmic ballet of alternate realities, alliances were tested. Trust, a fragile thread binding Elara and Felix, strained under the weight of the unknown. The unseen observer, their presence felt but unseen, continued to cast a shadow over their journey, leaving cryptic clues that hinted at a purpose beyond mere observation.

In the heart of a quantum convergence, where multiple realities intersected, Elara and Felix confronted a crossroads. The Quantum Navigator flickered, its stability faltering. The entanglement fields, pushed to their limits, quivered with uncertainty. In that critical moment, Elara faced a choice – to retreat to the safety of her known reality or to push forward into the abyss of the quantum unknown.

As the Quantum Navigator's glow intensified, casting a kaleidoscope of colors around them, Elara's decision rippled through the entanglement fields, setting in motion events that would reshape the very foundations of their understanding. The entangled alliances forged in the quantum realms held the promise of revelation, but with revelation came the inevitable descent into the quantum unknown, where the boundaries between discovery and danger blurred like the shifting sands of a cosmic desert.

5

Whispers of Betrayal

The Quantum Navigator hummed with an otherworldly resonance as Elara and Felix emerged from the quantum corridor into a realm bathed in a surreal, shifting twilight. The air crackled with an unsettling energy, and the landscape before them seemed to ripple with an ominous vibrancy.

Felix's eyes narrowed, a flicker of uncertainty crossing his features. "Elara, we've entered a reality on the brink of collapse. The entanglement fields here are inherently unstable."

The landscape resembled a fractured dreamscape, where reality warped and twisted in surreal contortions. As they ventured further, the whispers of an impending cataclysm grew louder, carried by ethereal winds that rustled through the distorted foliage.

Amidst the dissonance, a figure emerged from the shadows – a silhouette against the shifting hues of the alien sky. Dr. Marcus Turner, Elara's colleague from the quantum lab, stood before them. His eyes, once trustworthy, now harbored a glint of deception.

"Marcus? How did you…?" Elara began, her voice trailing off as Marcus raised a hand, a disarming smile playing on his lips.

"I followed your trail, Elara. The Quantum Navigator's disturbances couldn't escape my notice. But I see you've found yourself a companion in Dr. Arden," Marcus remarked, his words dripping with a calculated nonchalance.

Felix regarded Marcus with a scrutinizing gaze, his instincts sensing an underlying tension. "You're not telling us everything, Marcus. What brought you to this realm, and why the secrecy?"

Marcus hesitated, his eyes darting between Elara and Felix. "The Quantum Navigator can be a tool for great power. I couldn't risk its potential falling into the wrong hands. I had to ensure its responsible use."

Elara, torn between trust and suspicion, felt the weight of an impending betrayal. The entanglement fields whispered warnings, their subtle vibrations resonating with a sense of impending doom. The delicate threads of their alliance strained as Marcus's true motives remained veiled in shadows.

As they journeyed deeper into the fractured reality, Marcus led them to a structure at the heart of the distorted landscape – a quantum observatory pulsating with an eerie glow. Symbols of unknown origin adorned its walls, and the air thrummed with an unsettling resonance.

"This observatory is a nexus point of quantum energies," Marcus explained, his demeanor shifting to a mix of urgency and determination. "Here, we can harness the unstable entanglement fields to glimpse into the very fabric of existence."

Elara's skepticism grew, her trust in Marcus waning. The observatory, a convergence of ancient knowledge and quantum manipulation, felt like a crossroads where destinies collided. Felix, sensing the tension, voiced his concerns.

"We tread on precarious ground, Elara. Marcus's motives are shrouded, and the very foundations of this reality quake with uncertainty. Be cautious; the whispers of betrayal linger in the air."

As the trio approached the observatory's core, the Quantum Navigator pulsated in tandem with the ominous hum emanating from the structure. Reality itself seemed to fracture, revealing glimpses of shadowy figures moving in the periphery.

In a sudden twist, Marcus turned, a malevolent glint in his eyes. "Elara, the power of the Quantum Navigator is not meant for the timid. Embrace the unknown, for it holds the key to unlocking the secrets of the multiverse."

The observatory's glow intensified, casting long shadows that danced with treacherous intent. Elara stood at the precipice of a revelation, torn between alliances and the haunting whispers of betrayal. The entanglement fields quivered, and as Marcus's true agenda unfolded, the delicate threads of trust unraveled in the face of impending danger, plunging them into the depths of a reality on the verge of collapse.

6

Quantum Shadows

The observatory's pulsating glow cast elongated shadows that danced in ominous synchrony with the humming Quantum Navigator. Elara stood at the nexus of uncertainty, caught between the cryptic motives of Marcus and the unsettling revelations of the fractured reality.

As the observatory's resonance intensified, Felix's eyes narrowed with a mix of concern and determination. "Elara, this place resonates with an ancient energy, a force that transcends the known boundaries of quantum entanglement. We tread on the edge of cosmic mysteries, but beware, for mysteries often conceal unseen dangers."

The air crackled with anticipation as Marcus, now revealed as a player with his own agenda, approached a central console adorned with arcane symbols. He manipulated the Quantum Navigator with a sense of familiarity that raised unsettling questions about his true knowledge of these realms.

"Elara, the Quantum Navigator is a conduit to the shadows between realities. Embrace its power, and you can unlock the secrets that elude the grasp of conventional science," Marcus proclaimed, his voice echoing with a magnetic charisma that seemed to sway the very fabric of reality.

Elara, torn between trust and skepticism, contemplated the choices that lay before her. The Quantum Navigator, a gateway to the unknown, held the promise of enlightenment, but the shadows it cast whispered of untold dangers. Felix, sensing the delicate balance unraveling, urged caution.

"The quantum shadows conceal more than they reveal, Elara. Marcus's motives remain veiled, and the entanglement fields resonate with an unsettling dissonance. Trust your instincts, for the path we tread is fraught with uncertainty."

As Marcus initiated the Quantum Navigator, the observatory's glow intensified, casting an ethereal brilliance that bathed the room in a cosmic luminescence. Reality itself seemed to ripple as the entanglement fields responded to the manipulation of quantum energies.

In the midst of the luminous display, shadows coalesced into enigmatic figures – quantum echoes that defied conventional understanding. Elara felt an otherworldly presence, a chorus of whispers that reverberated through the observatory. The shadows, sentient and elusive, danced on the periphery of perception.

Felix, his gaze penetrating the veil between realities, murmured, "These quantum shadows are entities that defy our understanding. They exist at the intersection of possibility and impossibility, reflections of choices unmade and destinies unfulfilled."

The shadows, drawn to the Quantum Navigator's resonance, circled Elara and her companions. Their forms morphed, revealing glimpses of faces distorted by the quantum dance. The air pulsed with an ethereal energy that left an indelible imprint on the fabric of the observers' consciousness.

In the midst of this cosmic ballet, Marcus's eyes gleamed with an intensity that betrayed a deeper connection to the shadows. He seemed to commune with the entities, conversing in a language beyond the limits of human comprehension. Elara, grappling with the revelations unfolding before her, felt the boundaries between observer and observed blur.

As the shadows encircled them, an unsettling realization dawned on Elara – the Quantum Navigator wasn't merely a tool; it was a bridge to sentient entities that existed within the quantum tapestry. The observatory, a nexus of ancient knowledge and quantum manipulation, had become a stage where the players, human and shadow alike, converged in a cosmic drama of unraveling destinies.

Amidst the swirling shadows, a voice resonated – a synthesis of the whispers that danced through the entanglement fields. "Elara Quinn, the weaver of quantum destinies, embrace the shadows, for within them lies the key to understanding the enigma of your existence."

The observatory trembled, the Quantum Navigator's glow reaching a crescendo. Reality itself seemed to fracture, and as Elara faced the convergence of cosmic forces, the choices she made in this moment would resonate not only through the quantum shadows but echo through the very foundations of her reality.

7

Temporal Nexus

The observatory trembled as the Quantum Navigator's resonance reached a climax. The entangled shadows, sentient echoes of quantum possibilities, converged around Elara, Felix, and Marcus in a cosmic dance. The air pulsed with an ethereal energy that seemed to transcend the boundaries of time itself.

In the heart of the observatory, a rift in the fabric of reality manifested – a temporal nexus where the past, present, and future converged. Elara, captivated by the allure of the unknown, approached the rift with a mix of trepidation and fascination.

Felix, ever vigilant, cautioned, "Elara, the temporal nexus is a convergence point of temporal energies. Its existence defies the linear progression of time. Be wary, for the choices made here resonate across the tapestry of your existence."

Marcus, his eyes reflecting a calculated determination, approached the rift with an air of reverence. "The temporal nexus holds the key to unlocking the secrets of the Quantum Navigator. Embrace its power, and you can wield the forces that shape destinies."

As Elara stood at the threshold of the rift, the quantum shadows swirled around her, their forms merging and diverging in a kaleidoscopic display. The echoes of alternate timelines whispered through the temporal energies, offering glimpses of divergent paths and untold possibilities.

The observatory's glow intensified, casting long shadows that stretched across the cosmic landscape. The air crackled with an otherworldly resonance, and Elara felt a gravitational pull toward the nexus, as if the very fabric of time sought to draw her into its enigmatic embrace.

With a hesitant step, Elara crossed the threshold, and the temporal energies enveloped her. Visions unfolded before her eyes – scenes from her own past, present, and futures that diverged like branching pathways. She witnessed pivotal moments, choices made and unmade, and the consequences that rippled through the quantum tapestry.

In one timeline, she glimpsed a version of herself achieving unparalleled success in the realm of quantum physics, unlocking the secrets of the entanglement fields for the betterment of humanity. In another, a darker path unfolded – a reality marred by the misuse of quantum power, leading to catastrophic consequences.

The quantum shadows whispered cryptic messages, their voices blending into a harmonious symphony of temporal echoes. "Elara Quinn, the weaver of possibilities, the choices you make resonate across the quantum realms. The temporal nexus is a reflection of your agency within the cosmic tapestry."

As Elara navigated the temporal currents, a revelation struck her – the unseen observer, the mysterious voice, and the shadows themselves were manifestations of her own influence on the quantum fabric. The observatory, the Quantum Navigator, and the temporal nexus were instruments through which she explored the intricate threads of her own existence.

Felix, observing the unfolding spectacle, recognized the gravity of the moment. "Elara, the nexus is a crossroads where the paths of your potential selves intersect. The choices you make here will define not only your journey but the very nature of the quantum reality we inhabit."

In the midst of the temporal nexus, Marcus's demeanor shifted. His gaze, once filled with conviction, now harbored a glint of uncertainty. "Elara, the power to shape destinies lies within your grasp. Embrace it, and together we can transcend the limitations of mortal existence."

As the rift pulsed with temporal energies, Elara faced a pivotal decision – to wield the Quantum Navigator's power for enlightenment or to resist the allure and maintain the delicate balance of the quantum realms. The shadows, swirling with anticipation, awaited her choice, and the echoes of alternate timelines reverberated through the cosmic tapestry.

The observatory trembled, and Elara's decision rippled through the quantum shadows. The temporal nexus, a convergence of past, present, and future, held its breath as the weaver of possibilities faced the crossroads of her own existence. The entangled destinies, suspended in the delicate balance of the quantum dance, awaited the revelation that would shape the course of their intertwined fates.

8

Infinite Echoes

The temporal nexus quivered as Elara Quinn confronted the pivotal choice within its ethereal embrace. The quantum shadows, sentient echoes of possibilities, whispered through the cosmic symphony, their voices a delicate harmony that resonated with the tapestry of time.

As Elara stood at the nexus, her gaze shifted between the divergent pathways unfolding before her. The Quantum Navigator pulsed in synchrony with her heartbeat, its glow casting an otherworldly brilliance across the cosmic landscape. The echoes of alternate timelines played out like a mesmerizing dance, each step a potential divergence in the infinite tapestry of existence.

Felix, a stalwart companion in the quantum odyssey, observed with a blend of concern and curiosity. "Elara, the nexus holds the reflections of your choices, a mosaic of destinies that span the breadth of the quantum multiverse. Your decision here transcends the boundaries of individual timelines; it influences the very fabric of our shared reality."

Marcus, once a mysterious guide, now watched with an enigmatic gaze that betrayed the uncertainty within him. "Elara, embrace the power of the Quantum Navigator. Become the architect of infinite possibilities. Together, we can reshape the quantum realms and transcend the limitations of mortal understanding."

The echoes of Marcus's words reverberated through Elara's mind. The allure of wielding the Quantum Navigator's power, of unraveling the mysteries that lay beyond the veil of the known, beckoned to her. Yet, within the shadows of the nexus, a sense of caution whispered through the entangled threads of her consciousness.

As she contemplated her choice, a new voice resonated through the temporal energies. The unseen observer, shrouded in quantum ambiguity, spoke with a cadence that transcended the limitations of vocal expression. "Elara Quinn, the choices you make here echo through the corridors of time. The Quantum Navigator is a double-edged sword, a conduit to enlightenment and a harbinger of unforeseen consequences."

The cosmic dance of the quantum shadows intensified, their forms merging and diverging in a hypnotic display. Visions of potential futures overlapped and intertwined, creating a kaleidoscope of temporal possibilities. Elara felt the weight of responsibility as she stood at the nexus, a weaver of destinies caught between the threads of the quantum dance.

In one vision, she glimpsed a future where the Quantum Navigator's power was harnessed for benevolent purposes – a beacon of enlightenment guiding humanity towards new frontiers of understanding. In another, a darker path unfolded, where the unchecked manipulation of quantum energies led to cataclysmic events, unraveling the very fabric of reality.

The entangled destinies urged Elara to consider the consequences of her actions. The quantum shadows, once elusive echoes, seemed to converge, their collective presence transcending individuality. They whispered with a unified voice, "Choose wisely, for the echoes of your decision resonate not only through the quantum realms but echo through the corridors of your own soul."

As Elara grappled with the magnitude of her choice, the temporal energies pulsed with increasing intensity. The Quantum Navigator's glow radiated with a cosmic luminescence that mirrored the possibilities before her. The unseen observer, a silent witness to the quantum symphony, lingered in the shadows, their enigmatic presence leaving an indelible imprint on the unfolding narrative.

Felix, recognizing the weight of the moment, offered a steady reassurance. "Elara, the quantum realms are a delicate balance of possibilities. Your choices shape not only the future but define the essence of our reality. Trust your instincts, for the heart of the quantum dance beats within you."

With a deep breath, Elara made her decision. The Quantum Navigator responded to the resonance of her intent, and the temporal nexus pulsed with the echoes of her chosen path. The quantum shadows, in a final cosmic flourish, dispersed into the tapestry of time, carrying the ripples of her decision across the entangled destinies.

As the observatory settled into a serene stillness, Elara faced the unknown future she had woven. The Quantum Navigator, now a vessel of her chosen destiny, held the promise of enlightenment and the burden of responsibility. The entangled destinies awaited the unfolding narrative, and within the quantum realms, the echoes of Elara's choice resonated through the infinite corridors of possibility.

9

Fractured Realities

The aftermath of Elara's choice hung in the air like the lingering vibrations of a cosmic symphony. The temporal nexus, having witnessed the echoes of divergent destinies, settled into a quiet resonance. The Quantum Navigator, now attuned to Elara's chosen path, pulsed with a subdued glow.

Felix, his eyes reflecting a mix of curiosity and concern, broke the silence that enveloped the observatory. "Elara, the quantum realms are in flux. The echoes of your decision ripple through the entangled destinies. What path have you set into motion?"

Elara, still grappling with the weight of her choice, regarded the Quantum Navigator with a mix of awe and trepidation. "I've chosen to wield its power for enlightenment, to explore the mysteries of the quantum realms while safeguarding the delicate balance of reality."

Marcus, his enigmatic gaze lingering in the shadows, nodded with a sense of approval. "A choice made with conviction. The Quantum Navigator is a vessel of infinite potential, and with it, we can unravel the secrets that elude the grasp of conventional understanding."

As the trio contemplated the unfolding narrative, a disturbance echoed through the observatory. The very fabric of reality seemed to warp and twist, creating a dissonance that sent shivers through the quantum tapestry. The unseen observer, their presence hinted at by the lingering shadows, revealed themselves with an ethereal resonance.

"Elara Quinn, the weaver of destinies, your choice reverberates through the quantum realms. But beware, for enlightenment comes with a price. The delicate threads of reality may fray, and the boundaries between certainty and uncertainty may blur," the unseen observer intoned, their voice carrying a weight that transcended the limitations of mortal comprehension.

As the observatory quivered, the Quantum Navigator emitted a pulsating hum, as if acknowledging the unseen observer's cryptic warning. The entangled destinies, still settling into the new narrative, awaited the consequences of Elara's chosen path.

In the wake of the disturbance, anomalies manifested within the observatory. Quantum fluctuations, once controlled and predictable, now danced with a chaotic fervor. Holographic displays flickered, revealing glimpses of alternate realities bleeding into the fabric of the known.

Felix, his scientific instincts tingling with unease, analyzed the data streams. "Elara, your choice has disrupted the stability of the entanglement fields. The quantum fluctuations suggest a convergence of realities, a merging of possibilities that transcends the expected outcomes."

The observatory's glow intensified, casting long shadows that seemed to writhe with a sentience of their own. The unseen observer, their presence now palpable, spoke with a resonance that mirrored the shifting energies within the observatory.

"The Quantum Navigator, a vessel of enlightenment, has become a bridge between realities. The entangled destinies converge, creating a tapestry where the boundaries between alternate worlds blur," the unseen observer revealed, their cryptic words hinting at a cosmic convergence beyond Elara's control.

As the observatory continued to resonate with quantum energies, a portal manifested at its core – a swirling vortex of shimmering lights that defied the known laws of physics. The convergence of realities reached a climax, and the quantum shadows, once distinct echoes, merged into a unified presence that cast a spectral glow across the observatory.

Elara, Felix, and Marcus found themselves at the threshold of the portal, its cosmic allure beckoning them toward the unknown. The unseen observer, their form now revealed as a shimmering silhouette within the quantum shadows, spoke with a haunting cadence.

"Step into the quantum convergence, for the boundaries between realities have become permeable. The choices made within this cosmic dance will shape not only your destinies but the very essence of the entangled multiverse."

With a shared glance, Elara, Felix, and Marcus approached the portal. The Quantum Navigator, now a beacon of infinite potential, pulsed with the energies of enlightenment and uncertainty. As they crossed the threshold, reality itself seemed to fracture, and the observatory dissolved into a cosmic kaleidoscope of swirling lights.

In the heart of the quantum convergence, Elara and her companions faced a journey into the unknown – a cosmic odyssey where the boundaries between observer and observed, reality and possibility, would blur into a tapestry of infinite echoes. The entangled destinies, guided by the choices made within the quantum dance, awaited the revelation of what lay beyond the fractured realities that unfolded before them.

10

Ephemeral Horizons

The quantum convergence enveloped Elara, Felix, and Marcus in a maelstrom of cosmic energies. Lights of indescribable hues danced around them, casting an ethereal glow on the fabric of their reality. The observatory, now a distant memory, dissolved into the luminous currents of the quantum convergence.

As the trio traversed the swirling vortex, the boundaries between observer and observed blurred. They became spectral entities within the cosmic dance, their forms ephemeral and indistinct. The Quantum Navigator, held tightly by Elara, pulsed with a rhythmic resonance that harmonized with the cosmic symphony surrounding them.

The unseen observer, a shimmering silhouette within the quantum shadows, guided them through the kaleidoscopic expanse. "Welcome to the ephemeral horizons, where the entangled destinies converge and alternate realities intermingle. The choices made within this cosmic odyssey shape the very fabric of the quantum multiverse."

Reality itself seemed to ripple as they ventured deeper into the quantum convergence. Glimpses of alternate worlds flickered like fleeting dreams, each a possibility entwined within the cosmic tapestry. The quantum shadows, once distinct echoes, merged into a collective presence that watched with a silent knowing.

Felix, his scientific curiosity tinged with a sense of reverence, marveled at the shifting vistas. "This transcends the boundaries of conventional understanding. We are witnesses to the interconnected threads of the entangled multiverse, where possibilities intertwine in a cosmic dance."

Marcus, his enigmatic demeanor hinting at a deeper understanding, nodded in agreement. "Elara, the Quantum Navigator has opened a gateway to the ephemeral horizons. We stand at the nexus of infinite potential, where the choices we make echo through the quantum realms."

Elara, holding the Quantum Navigator aloft, felt the weight of responsibility. The choices that had led them to this cosmic convergence, the weaving of destinies within the quantum dance, unfolded before her like a cosmic tapestry. The unseen observer, their presence resonating within the quantum shadows, spoke with a voice that echoed through the expanse.

"The entangled destinies converge here, and the ephemeral horizons are the canvas upon which your choices are painted. Embrace the cosmic dance, for within its rhythms lies the key to understanding the ever-shifting nature of existence."

As they journeyed through the ephemeral horizons, the quantum convergence presented them with surreal landscapes. In one reality, a city of crystalline structures floated amidst the clouds, harnessing quantum energies for harmonious coexistence. In another, a desolate wasteland echoed with the remnants of a technological apocalypse, a cautionary tale of unchecked quantum manipulation.

The quantum shadows, now a spectral chorus, whispered enigmatic messages. "Choices ripple through the tapestry, leaving imprints on the very fabric of reality. The ephemeral horizons are the meeting point of divergent destinies, where alternate worlds converge and entwine."

In the heart of the cosmic dance, a pivotal moment awaited. A nexus within the ephemeral horizons, where the entangled destinies reached a crossroads. The unseen observer, their silhouette bathed in the shimmering lights, guided Elara, Felix, and Marcus toward a focal point where possibilities converged.

As they approached the nexus, a revelation unfolded – the ephemeral horizons were not merely a canvas for observation but a crucible of creation. The Quantum Navigator, now a conduit of their collective will, pulsed with an intensity that mirrored the cosmic energies surrounding them.

The unseen observer spoke with a resonant certainty, "At this nexus, shape the destiny you seek. The quantum realms respond to the choices made within the ephemeral horizons. Will you be architects of enlightenment or harbingers of cosmic upheaval?"

Elara, Felix, and Marcus faced a choice that transcended individual desires. The cosmic convergence, a nexus of infinite potential, awaited the imprint of their collective will. The Quantum Navigator, a vessel of enlightenment and uncertainty, pulsed with a cosmic luminescence that reflected the weight of their decisions.

With a shared determination, they extended their hands toward the focal point of the nexus. The quantum shadows, now a luminous chorus, merged into a celestial crescendo that echoed through the ephemeral horizons.

Reality itself seemed to tremble as the choices made within the cosmic dance rippled through the entangled multiverse. The quantum convergence, a tapestry woven with the threads of their decisions, resonated with a harmonious symphony that transcended the limitations of mortal understanding.

As the ephemeral horizons embraced the imprints of their collective will, Elara, Felix, and Marcus became integral to the cosmic dance. The quantum shadows, now a vibrant echo, whispered cryptic messages that hinted at the unfolding narrative within the entangled multiverse.

The unseen observer, their silhouette merging with the luminous currents, intoned with a final resonance, "Ephemeral horizons weave the stories of existence. The cosmic dance continues, and within its rhythms, the entangled destinies embark on a journey through the ever-shifting tapestry of the quantum realms."

11

Resonance of Choices

Within the ephemeral horizons, Elara, Felix, and Marcus stood at the nexus of infinite potential. The quantum convergence, a cosmic crucible where choices resonated through the entangled multiverse, pulsated with an otherworldly luminescence. The Quantum Navigator, held aloft by Elara, hummed in tandem with the cosmic energies that surrounded them.

The unseen observer, now an integral part of the luminous currents within the quantum shadows, guided them toward a focal point where destinies converged. Their voice, a harmonious blend of echoes and whispers, resonated with a cosmic certainty.

"At the nexus of choices, the entangled destinies converge. The Quantum Navigator, now attuned to your collective will, is the vessel through which your chosen destinies will unfold. Shape the narrative of the quantum realms with the resonance of your decisions."

As they approached the focal point, the luminous currents shifted, revealing glimpses of alternate realities that coalesced in a cosmic tapestry. Elara, Felix, and Marcus glimpsed moments that mirrored their past, present, and potential futures. The choices made within the quantum dance echoed through the ephemeral horizons, creating a symphony of intertwined destinies.

Felix, his gaze scanning the cosmic tapestry, spoke with a sense of wonder. "The resonance of our choices is woven into the very fabric of existence. Each decision, a thread within the quantum tapestry, creates a harmonious interplay of destinies."

Marcus, his enigmatic demeanor hinting at a deeper understanding, nodded in agreement. "The Quantum Navigator is a conduit through which our collective will shapes the cosmic dance. Let our choices be the guiding notes in the symphony of the entangled multiverse."

As they reached the focal point, a convergence of energies manifested – a swirling vortex of lights that seemed to transcend the boundaries of space and time. The quantum shadows, now a luminous chorus, whispered enigmatic messages that guided Elara, Felix, and Marcus in their next steps.

The unseen observer intoned with a resonant certainty, "Within this cosmic vortex, the entangled destinies await your imprint. The Quantum Navigator, now a vessel of collective will, will channel your chosen path into the quantum realms. Embrace the resonance of your decisions, for within them lies the essence of the quantum dance."

With shared determination, Elara, Felix, and Marcus extended their hands toward the cosmic vortex. The Quantum Navigator, responsive to the energy of their collective will, emitted a radiant glow that synchronized with the luminous currents around them.

Reality itself seemed to warp as they stepped into the cosmic vortex. The quantum shadows, now a vibrant echo, enveloped them in a cascade of shimmering lights. The ephemeral horizons shifted, and the nexus of choices unfolded into a surreal expanse where alternate realities converged.

As they journeyed through the cosmic vortex, moments from their past, present, and potential futures played out in a mesmerizing display. Elara witnessed a reality where her quantum research led to groundbreaking discoveries, shaping the course of scientific understanding. Felix glimpsed a version of himself immersed in a realm of quantum harmonics, unlocking the mysteries of the cosmic frequencies.

Marcus, his enigmatic presence resonating within the quantum realms, observed scenes that hinted at a deeper connection to the cosmic dance. The entangled destinies, now a tapestry of intertwined narratives, pulsed with the vibrancy of their collective choices.

In the heart of the cosmic vortex, a pivotal moment awaited. The unseen observer, their luminous silhouette guiding the way, spoke with a voice that echoed through the quantum realms. "At the nexus of destinies, let your choices become the echoes that reverberate through the entangled multiverse. The cosmic dance awaits the imprint of your will."

As they reached the culmination of the cosmic vortex, the luminous currents converged into a focal point where destinies intertwined. The Quantum Navigator, now a beacon of their chosen path, emitted a brilliant glow that resonated with the symphony of the quantum dance.

With a shared intent, Elara, Felix, and Marcus channeled their collective will into the Quantum Navigator. Reality itself seemed to shift as the chosen destinies unfolded within the cosmic expanse. The luminous currents embraced the resonance of their decisions, weaving a narrative that transcended the limitations of mortal understanding.

As the cosmic vortex dissipated, Elara, Felix, and Marcus found themselves in a reality transformed by the echoes of their choices. The quantum shadows, now a radiant echo, surrounded them in a cosmic embrace. The ephemeral horizons, still shimmering with the vibrancy of the quantum dance, awaited the unfolding narrative shaped by the resonance of their decisions.

The unseen observer, their luminous presence lingering within the quantum shadows, spoke with a final resonance. "Ephemeral horizons weave the stories of existence. The entangled destinies, now intertwined by the resonance of your choices, embark on a journey through the ever-shifting tapestry of the quantum realms."

As Elara, Felix, and Marcus stood in the transformed reality, the Quantum Navigator in their grasp, they faced the unknown with a profound awareness. The choices made within the cosmic dance had become the echoes that shaped their destinies, and the entangled multiverse awaited the unfolding narrative that resonated with the vibrancy of their collective will.

12

Harmony of Echoes

The transformed reality embraced Elara, Felix, and Marcus in the aftermath of the cosmic vortex. The Quantum Navigator, now a conduit of their collective will, pulsed with a serene glow that reflected the resonance of their chosen destinies. The quantum shadows, a luminous echo, surrounded them in a cosmic symphony that transcended the boundaries of ordinary perception.

As they surveyed the altered landscape, remnants of alternate realities merged seamlessly into the fabric of their transformed world. The ephemeral horizons, still shimmering with the vibrancy of the quantum dance, hinted at the entangled destinies woven by the resonance of their decisions.

Felix, ever the scientist, marveled at the changes. "The boundaries between realities have blurred, creating a tapestry where echoes of alternate worlds harmonize in a cosmic symphony. We are witnesses to the transformative power of the Quantum Navigator."

Elara, holding the Quantum Navigator with a sense of reverence, felt the weight of responsibility. "The choices we made within the cosmic vortex have shaped this reality. The entangled destinies now coexist in a harmonious interplay, guided by the echoes of our collective will."

Marcus, his enigmatic demeanor hinting at a deeper understanding, observed the cosmic landscape. "The Quantum Navigator has become a vessel of harmony, channeling the resonance of our decisions into the fabric of this transformed reality. We have become architects of a new cosmic narrative."

The unseen observer, their luminous presence still lingering within the quantum shadows, spoke with a voice that echoed through the altered landscape. "The cosmic dance continues, and within the harmony of echoes, the entangled destinies find balance. The Quantum Navigator, now a beacon of unity, guides the weave of existence."

As they ventured deeper into the transformed reality, the quantum shadows whispered cryptic messages. "The entangled multiverse has found equilibrium. The echoes of alternate worlds coalesce into a cosmic tapestry, each thread harmonizing with the others in a dance of interconnected destinies."

The landscape revealed moments from their altered past, present, and potential futures. Scenes played out like surreal vignettes – Elara achieving unprecedented breakthroughs in quantum research, Felix unraveling the mysteries of cosmic frequencies, and Marcus navigating the enigmatic realms of the quantum dance.

In the heart of the transformed reality, a nexus of cosmic convergence awaited. The Quantum Navigator, attuned to the resonance of their collective will, led them toward a focal point where destinies intersected. The luminous currents, still vibrant with the energies of the quantum dance, guided them to the culmination of their journey.

As they reached the nexus, the quantum shadows converged, forming a luminous chorus that enveloped them in a celestial embrace. The unseen observer, their silhouette now a radiant presence within the cosmic symphony, spoke with a final resonance.

"At the nexus of destinies, the entangled multiverse finds equilibrium. The Quantum Navigator, now a vessel of unity, weaves the threads of existence into a harmonious tapestry. Your choices, resonating through the cosmic dance, have become the echoes that guide the harmony of interconnected destinies."

With a shared understanding, Elara, Felix, and Marcus extended their hands toward the focal point. The Quantum Navigator, responsive to the collective will, emitted a radiant glow that synchronized with the luminous currents around them.

Reality itself seemed to shift as they stepped into the nexus. The cosmic symphony reached a crescendo, and the quantum shadows, now a celestial chorus, harmonized with the vibrancy of the quantum dance. The transformed reality embraced the resonance of their decisions, creating a nexus where destinies intertwined in a dance of cosmic unity.

As the luminous currents settled, the transformed reality revealed a harmonious coexistence of alternate worlds. The entangled destinies, once divergent threads, now merged into a cosmic tapestry that transcended the limitations of individual timelines.

The unseen observer, their radiant presence lingering within the quantum shadows, spoke with a final assurance. "The cosmic dance continues, guided by the resonance of your choices. The entangled multiverse, now a tapestry of harmonized destinies, embarks on a journey through the ever-shifting fabric of existence."

Elara, Felix, and Marcus stood as witnesses to the transformed reality they had shaped. The Quantum Navigator, now a symbol of unity, held the essence of their collective will. The quantum shadows, a celestial chorus, whispered a final echo that lingered in the cosmic symphony.

As they gazed upon the harmonized tapestry of existence, the entangled destinies interwoven in a dance of cosmic unity, Elara, Felix, and Marcus faced the unknown future with a profound awareness. The Quantum Navigator, now a beacon of harmony, pulsed with the vibrancy of the cosmic dance.

In the heart of the transformed reality, where echoes of alternate worlds harmonized in a cosmic symphony, the entangled multiverse embraced a new narrative shaped by the resonance of their collective will. The journey through the quantum realms had become a timeless odyssey, and within the harmony of echoes, the entangled destinies embarked on a cosmic dance through the ever-shifting fabric of existence.

Milton Keynes UK
Ingram Content Group UK Ltd.
UKHW020612071223
433828UK00014B/733